Classic Tales

Level 2

M000305221

Jack and the Beanstalk

Retold by Sue Arengo
Illustrated by Alejandro O'Kif

 Contents

OXFORD
UNIVERSITY PRESS

 'We've got no food, Jack,' says his mother. 'We've got no money. Go and sell the cow!'

We've got no food.

So Jack goes up the road.

'Look!' says a strange old man. 'Magic beans! Give me that cow and you can have them!'

'Oh!' says Jack. 'All right!'

Magic beans!

'What?' shouts Jack's mother. 'No money? Beans! Go to bed now!'

But in the morning there's a beanstalk!

Tall, tall, tall … And green … green … green!

'Oooh!' says Jack. 'Wonderful! Magic!'

Wonderful! Magic!

Jack climbs out of the window. He climbs up the beanstalk. Up … up … up.

Jack comes to a road. He walks and walks.

Then he sees a house – a big, big house. And a woman – a big, big woman.

'Can I have some breakfast?'
says Jack.

'All right!' she says. 'Come in.
But listen! My man is a giant.
He eats boys. So be quiet!'

She gives Jack some breakfast.

Then there's a noise. Thump!
Thump! Thump!

'My big man is here!' she says.
'Quick! Hide! Get in there!'

'Fee! Fi! Fo! Foy! I can smell a little boy!' says the big giant.

'No, you can't!' says his wife. 'Wash your hands! Your breakfast is ready!'

He eats his breakfast. Then he says, 'Wife! Bring me my gold!'

He puts the gold on the table. 'One … two … three … Zzzzz.'

The giant goes to sleep.

Then Jack comes out quietly. He takes a bag of gold. And quietly he runs away.

Jack runs back down the long road. He climbs back down the beanstalk. And he takes the gold home to his mother.

'Look, Mother! Look!' he says.

Look, Mother! Look!

Now they live well. But one day there's no more gold.

So Jack climbs up the beanstalk again. Up ... up ... up.

He comes to the road again. He walks and walks.

He sees the house again – the big, big house.

'Can I have some breakfast?' Jack says.

'Go away!' says the big woman. 'My big man eats boys. And you're a bad boy. You take things, don't you?'

Go away!

'I don't take things,' says Jack. 'That's another boy. I can tell you his name. But I want some breakfast first.'

'All right,' says the woman. 'Come in.'

She gives Jack some breakfast.

Then there's a noise. Thump! Thump! Thump!

'My big man is here!' says the woman. 'Quick! Hide! Get in there!'

Fee! Fi! Fo! Foy!

'Fee! Fi! Fo! Foy! I can smell a little boy!' says the giant.

'No, you can't!' says his wife. 'Wash your hands! Your breakfast is ready!'

After breakfast the giant says, 'Wife! Bring me my hen! I want some gold eggs!'

So she brings the hen to the table.

'Lay!' says the giant.

And the hen lays a gold egg.

'Yes!' says the giant. 'Lay! Lay!'

Then he goes to sleep.

Then Jack comes out. And he takes the magic hen. And he quietly runs away. He runs back home to his mother.

Jack and his mother are happy. They are never hungry now. But Jack wants to climb up the beanstalk one more time.

He comes to the road again. He walks and walks.

He sees the house again – the big, big house. And the woman – the big, big woman. But this time she doesn't see him.

Jack hides behind some books.

Soon he hears a noise.

'Fee! Fi! Fo! Foy! I can smell a little boy!' says the giant.

'Can you?' says his wife. 'Is that bad boy here again? Let's look in here. Perhaps he's hiding.'

But they can't find Jack.

Perhaps he's hiding.

After breakfast the giant says, 'Wife! Bring me my magic harp!'

She brings it and he says, 'Play, harp! Play!'

Then he goes to sleep.

Quietly Jack comes out. He takes the magic harp. And quietly he runs away.

But the harp calls out, 'Giant! Giant! The boy is taking me!'

Then the giant opens his eyes.

The boy is taking me!

'Help!' says Jack. He runs away fast. He runs down the long road.

'He's taking me!' sings the harp.

'Stop!' shouts the giant. 'Bring back my harp!'

Jack gets to the beanstalk. Quickly he climbs down … down … down … down.

'Mother! Get the axe! Quick! The big giant is coming!'

Jack cuts down the beanstalk.
And the giant falls down!

His head hits the ground –
THUMP! And he is dead!

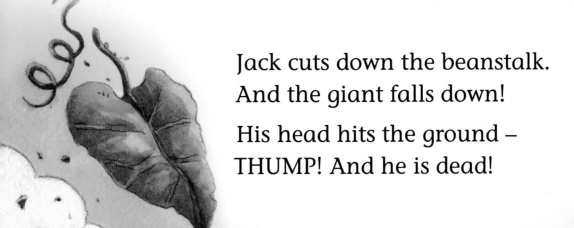

That's the end of him!

'That's the end of him!' says Jack.
'Now ... can I have some breakfast?'

Exercises

1 Write the words.

> brings ~~climbs~~ gives lays runs sees

1 Jack __climbs__ up the beanstalk.
2 He _____ a big, big woman.
3 The giant woman _____ him some breakfast.
4 She _____ a hen to the table.
5 The hen _____ a gold egg.
6 Jack _____ away with the hen.

2 What do they say? Write the words.

1 Look! Magic __beans__ !

2 Quick! _____ !

3 _____ your hands!

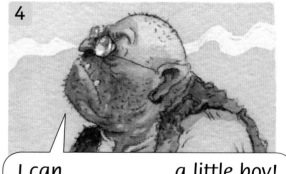

4 I can _____ a little boy!

3 Put the words in the correct order.

1 and cow the Go sell.

Go and sell the cow.

2 have breakfast Can some I?

_____

3 the Jack of climbs window out.

_____

4 boys My man big eats.

_____

4 Write the story again, correcting the mistake in each sentence.

Jack and his father have no food. Jack sells
the cow for some money. In the morning
Jack climbs down a beanstalk. A giant man
makes him breakfast. Jack takes some gold,
a cow, and a harp from the giant man. The giant
sings, 'Stop!' Jack runs away and cuts down
the tree. The giant climbs down.

Jack and his mother have no food.

_____

_____

_____

_____

_____

_____

Picture Dictionary

axe

breakfast

climb

cow

cut down

dead *He is dead.*

egg

fall down

giant

gold

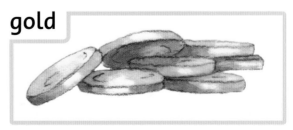

harp

hen

hide

lay

noise

road

run away

sell

shout

smell

wash

wife

Classic Tales

Classic stories retold for learners of English – bringing the magic of traditional storytelling to the language classroom

Level 1: 100 headwords
- The Enormous Turnip
- The Little Red Hen
- Lownu Mends the Sky
- The Magic Cooking Pot
- Mansour and the Donkey
- Peach Boy
- The Princess and the Pea
- Rumplestiltskin
- The Shoemaker and the Elves
- Three Billy-Goats

Level 2: 150 headwords
- Amrita and the Trees
- Big Baby Finn
- The Fisherman and his Wife
- The Gingerbread Man
- Jack and the Beanstalk
- Thumbelina
- The Town Mouse and the Country Mouse
- The Ugly Duckling

Level 3: 200 headwords
- Aladdin
- Goldilocks and the Three Bears
- The Little Mermaid
- Little Red Riding Hood

Level 4: 300 headwords
- Cinderella
- The Goose Girl
- Sleeping Beauty
- The Twelve Dancing Princesses

Level 5: 400 headwords
- Beauty and the Beast
- The Magic Brocade
- Pinocchio
- Snow White and the Seven Dwarfs

All *Classic Tales* have an accompanying
- **e-Book with Audio Pack** containing the book and the e-book with audio, for use on a computer or CD player. Teachers can also project the e-book onto an interactive whiteboard to use it like a Big Book.
- **Activity Book and Play** providing extra language practice and the story adapted as a play for performance in class or on stage.

For more details, visit
www.oup.com/elt/readers/classictales

OXFORD
UNIVERSITY PRESS

Great Clarendon Street, Oxford OX2 6DP

Oxford University Press is a department of the University of Oxford. It furthers the University's objective of excellence in research, scholarship, and education by publishing worldwide in

Oxford New York

Auckland Cape Town Dar es Salaam Hong Kong Karachi
Kuala Lumpur Madrid Melbourne Mexico City Nairobi
New Delhi Shanghai Taipei Toronto

With offices in

Argentina Austria Brazil Chile Czech Republic France Greece
Guatemala Hungary Italy Japan Poland Portugal Singapore
South Korea Switzerland Thailand Turkey Ukraine Vietnam

OXFORD and OXFORD ENGLISH are registered trade marks of Oxford University Press in the UK and in certain other countries

This edition © Oxford University Press 2011

The moral rights of the author have been asserted

Database right Oxford University Press (maker)

First published in *Classic Tales* 2005

2015 2014 2013 2012 2011
10 9 8 7 6 5 4 3 2 1

ISBN: 978 0 19 423898 4

This *Classic Tale* title is available as an e-Book with Audio Pack
ISBN: 978 0 19 423901 1

Also available: Jack and the Beanstalk Activity Book and Play
ISBN: 978 0 19 423899 1

Printed in China

This book is printed on paper from certified and well-managed sources.

ACKNOWLEDGEMENTS
Illustrated by: Alejandro O'Kif/Shannon Associates